EQUALS
GREATNESS
MoPoetry
Phillips

All rights reserved. No part of this book may be reproduced in any form without permission in writing by the publisher, except in the case of brief quotations embodied in critical articles or reviews. For information, please contact MoPoetry Phillips by email @ 1mopoetry@gmail.com.

I have tried to recreate events, locales and conversations from my memories of them. In order to maintain their anonymity, in some instances, I have changed the names of individuals and places. I may have changed some identifying characteristics and details such as physical properties, occupations, and places of residence. Any resemblance to actual persons, living or dead, or actual events is purely coincidental.

Cover Designer, Editor, Retoucher: Sylvia L. Blalock

Author photo: Stephanie Nichole Schmerr of SNS Photography.

All other photos belong to the author.

Printed in the United States of America

ISBN: 9781078439770

Poetry can be found at the Library of Congress, MoPoetry Volume 1, Service request 1-6657905531; MoPoetry Volume 2, Service request 1-7192645311; MoPoetry Volume 3, Service request 1-7829226579; MoPoetry Volume 4, Service request 1-7827363081; and MoPoetry Volume 5, Service request # 1-7826765316.

Table of Contents

Dedication 7

Equals Greatness....a mini autobiography 12

My Way of Escape 34

Pre- Eulogy 35

Dreams 38

The Flower and the Bee   (Fable) 39

Poetry is Like... 43

Turn Pages into Palettes 45

Landscape at Dawn 49

In Honor of my Mother   (Prose) 50

Aunt Stella   (Short Story) 52

Mom's Hands 56

Chosen for the Fire 58

Midnight 60

My Near Miss 63

What I Should Not Say 67

Stone 68

Choice 71

Safehouse 76

Mayonnaise 78

Pain 79

Wounded Soldier 81

Surprise Ending	83
Not Just A Mother	85
The Chameleon	89
The End	91
What is Beautiful	95
Come Back Up (Short Story)	96
Eradication of Ventriloquy	100
"I, Too, am America 2019"	102
Harlem	105
A Black Woman in Corporate America	107
I Don't Want to be Black	109
February	112
No Longer Winning	116
Full and Free	118
Maybe	120
Child Proof (Prose)	122
Public Smile, Private Storm	124
Your Right Hand	127
Introspection	129
The Butterfly	131
Imitation	133
Register	136
Love	138
Love for God	140
Fantasy (Lyrical Intro)	142

Hindsight (Short Form)	143
Clear	144
Garden Test	145
While Waiting on You	147
Who I am, and Where We Stand	149
Rough Around the Edges	151
My Warrior	152
Young Love	155
True Love	157
Dear King	159
Letter to Black Fathers	162
Letter to My Teenage Son	164
The Holidays	166
Nighttime Praise	169
From Mere Clay	171
Intervention	173
Outrageous Hope	175
Believe	177
It Will Come	178
Draw Nigh	179
In Your Presence	181
Face to Face	183
He Visits Me	185
Healed While in Worship	187
Life's Circumstances	189

Dedication

I dedicate this book to God. Without your protection and predestined plan for my life, I would not have made it. To my children Taran, DeShanne, and Caleb; grandchildren Joshua, Skylar, and little peanut on the way, my goal is to teach you about dream intimacy. To my mother, Shree Phillips, my first example of strength. To my father, James Silver, who always tells me that he is proud of me. To the late, great Bishop Johnnie L. Johnson, who taught me God speaks poetically and prophetically. To my mentor/friend, Dr. Kris Yohe, who helped me through some very difficult times in college. To all the wonderful women at Women Writing for (a) Change, thanks for your encouragement and support. To my friend, Murder She Wrote a.k.a. Hollie Luv, it is always good to have a strong woman, who are crazy enough to believe what you believe.

Now to those who have personally been assigned to help me succeed, my three poetry coaches: To Ryan Gordon, who helped me overcome my feelings of inadequacies. You helped me through a paralyzing heartbreak and gave me pages of advice that I will cherish forever. To Author Ronald Williams, my dear friend, who gave me courage and inspiration to do this. To Joseph Brown, who has been a true friend and encourager. To my support network and all the people who believe in me enough to purchase this book, I am truly grateful.

Love,

MoPoetry Phillips

"Equals Greatness" is a perfectly balanced multi-genre book that contains the author's powerful mini-autobiography which gives her very honest and heartfelt account of her experience as a domestic violence survivor. It won an AWP Journal Entry nomination for the state of Kentucky in 2011. In addition, the book contains a combination of seventy poems and short stories that she has written since then. The subject matter reaches the entire spectrum from rape, incest, sexual and emotional violations, racism, empowerment, betrayal, love, body positivity, and faith. Her first published piece "Surprise Ending," published by the Voices Project touches on the very hard topic of parenting. Her social justice pieces speak of past and present injustices that helped to shape her beliefs as an activist. Her social justice poems " I Don't Want to be Black" and "Eradication of Ventriloquy" was published in May 2019 by SOS Art 2019. Her narrative poems tap into the African American oral tradition. Her lyrical poems are full of wisdom. The inspirational poems will encourage you, uplift your spirit, and increase your faith in God. You will enjoy this book from beginning to end.

Equals Greatness

Equals Greatness....a mini autobiography

As a child, I loved to watch my mother put puzzles together. I would walk past the table and analyze her technique. First, she would find all the outside corners. Then, she would separate the varied pieces of the puzzle into similar patterns. Finally, she carefully tried each for an adequate match. Every new piece was a wonderful addition that brought clarity to the final product; pictures of mountains, blue skies, birds, and trees. We were careful not to lose any pieces, because each was used to equal something much greater.

I watched my feet closely while I walked up the narrow stairway. "How may I help you?" she said. Her sharp tone caused me to lift my head in sadness. Something's wrong, I thought. I tried to imagine what was around the corner and what distracted her from noticing that I hadn't even made it into the room yet, but the coldness of her voice answered all my questions. I entered her office in silence and closed the door behind me. My presence agitated her. I wasn't there for a biblical debate. I was shattered; bruised underneath and embarrassingly broken. I'd promised myself that I would not let another man beat me. I would rather let the church put me in hell with their theology than to stay married to him.

"Some people will do whatever they need in order to be saved." These were the only words I could repeat. Everything else was a heated debate between my resistance and her insensitivity. She was supposed to be a church counselor, a licensed psychiatrist. I needed a diagnosis. I needed her to explain what had been happening to me for the last three years. After meeting with her, I needed to be told that what I remembered was not reality. My mind had been taken apart like small puzzle pieces. It lingered around hoping someone could unscramble the mess and reveal the true picture from the varied pieces of memories.

I wondered how we managed to live in the same city and never cross paths. He was my high school sweetheart. We were broken apart by jealous friends, but I never really let him go. I held onto him with all the things that I kept. Things put in a white box with red letters, marked "Memorabilia". Inside were all the cards from Lutz Flowers. Memories from days he showed up at my locker with yet another beautiful bouquet. I'd filed away all the letters he wrote me. A photo album held pictures of all the places we'd gone: concerts, down to the square, and walking hand in hand along the river. I even kept a pair of his underwear. They were my secret things. No one needed to know that I held onto them for sixteen years.

My first house looked like a place where a man should be. Outside was a half court and basketball hoop. At night, I'd stand outside thinking that I knew my husband was on the way. The girls and I were so used to living alone that we forgot the bathroom had a door. I started yelling from the bedroom, "Close the door. My husband is out here!" They would just laugh and shake their heads. We only lived there for a few weeks, but I finally got up the nerve to walk the white box to the trash. For the first time in my life, I was ready to give up on the dream of getting back together with him. The following week I found myself frantically searching the house for it. I couldn't believe I'd actually thrown it away.

Several weeks later someone from my past saw me working at the grocery store. "Have you seen him?" she said. "No, not since high school," I replied. In fact, I hadn't seen her either. I tried to forget my former days and hid from everyone by going to church almost every night. The person in line behind her switched registers, as if he knew it would be a long conversation. I told her that I had bought a house right around the corner, and that I was just working in the store at night. She couldn't believe it. She explained that he worked right across the street from the grocery store. She made me promise her that I would say hello.

Two months after buying the house and a few weeks after being persuaded by the woman in the grocery store, I finally worked up enough nerve to go into the barbershop where he worked. Soon, I was cooking and bringing his lunches in. He would come into the grocery store every shift that I worked. I was the first person that he talked to when he woke up. Night after night was spent on the phone with him. Our first night together broke eleven years of celibacy. That had to mean something. I wanted to make him feel special. I wanted him to feel as if God had put someone on reserve for him alone. Within six months we were married, but even those six months were full of signs I ignored. I tried to convince myself that I knew him and that I could trust him. Common sense warned, "How can you possibly know someone you have not seen in sixteen years?" He wasn't someone I actually loved and knew. It was a love that I'd nurtured through fond memories.

I quickly found out that he was not the same person. I allowed him to tailor my wants into whatever he needed. After all his alterations were done, I was gone. My body lived in a dark and dreadful place, but something inside of me crawled from underneath in search of light. While I packed, I reminded myself not to hold onto any of his things. I filed for divorce. I decided the last time he hit me was the last time.

It was a long and tiring journey. As I healed, I thought about words he had said. Words that I couldn't understand at the time. Then I remembered the look in his eyes. Not the look he'd give me when my heart would jump when we heard creaky sounds from the settling of the house. It was the look that asked, "Why did I do it?" I wanted to remember only the emotionless monster towering over me, gritting his teeth, throwing me around, and leaving me broken. But as fear started to decrease, so did he. Then, I was finally able to find answers for the question in his eyes.

He would work hard and come straight home from work. He was a good provider for me and the kids. To him, that alone was an endless list. For me, it wasn't enough. It bothered him that I wanted him to feel things he never felt, and to reveal things that were too deeply buried under the previous pains. He seemed to resent even hearing my voice. Over and over he asked me to explain what I needed, but he could not hear me. If I asked for simple things, even a night out together, he treated my words like injurious verbal disapprovals of him. It hurt him to know I didn't need him, and as the want of him faded, he hoarded hatred and accumulated years of pain.

I heard the car door slam from the bedroom window. He was home. Immediately, I was coated with an eager readiness to match my vivid anticipation. This was the only thing that was about me. Each deep thrust was a flirtatious smile. Every change of position was a walk in the park. His big hands firmly grasping my hair was a hand gently placed on my back and a sweet kiss on the neck. All the glorious things done to my body exchanged for things I really needed. One day, I admitted to myself that I was making love to pretend that I was in love. Trading the physical for more tangible things.

(status update)

The best gift a man can give a woman is the ability to love them without reservation, hesitation, or fear, because their commitment is to God, not to you.

I stood at the dresser opening and closing bottles of perfume that he bought me until my eyes began to run and my nose burned. Valentine's Day, Mother's Day, each representing a special occasion, but I hated receiving gifts. People normally give what they want you to have instead of what you need. One thing I learned as a child was the most infrequent gift given was love and time. My thoughts were interrupted when his cell phone began to ring. I picked it up and ran into the bathroom to scroll through the numbers. I was tired of him pretending he didn't hear it or turning it off when we were together. I wanted to feel that I was his wife, but something told me I was just another woman to him.

"I don't care if his phone rings until it falls off the dresser. That is his business!" the pastor instructed. "You are one step away from paranoia," his wife chimed in. Just another marriage counseling session that made me look crazy and gave him more excuses. It didn't matter that I found a text from another woman saying she loved him, pornographic jokes sent back and forth between so-called friends, a text to me saying he was thinking of me, followed by a text to someone else saying he was thinking of them. I stood there unscathed while he pulled back his shirt to reveal the scratches, I'd given him. He didn't bother saying that he got them when he effortlessly moved my wedged body from against the bathroom door to recover his phone. He didn't explain how he broke it to keep me from calling her back. He cried and told them he would do anything to make the marriage work. Meanwhile, I sat there silently in disbelief. After changing his number three times, the calls still came. Part of me wanted to find male friends that I could talk to so that I could rub it in his face, but I did something worse. I grew numb out of loss of respect for him.

Day after day, I would hear his complaints. Complaints about work. Complaints about the children. "Do you ever call to say I love you, or talk about anything else?" I asked. Our phone calls to each other began to get shorter and shorter. Every day, I was drained by the cursing, yelling, and the anger in his voice. Seeing him in person didn't help either. He talked to me as a father scolding his child.

I recognized the disapproving look of his clenched lips, but I also recognized something else, the rage.

(status update)

Cry, scream, or go into spiritual warfare. Please do not respond unless you know where I am right now.

Blood finger painted an abstract painting on the wall. The horribleness of it was seen in my son's eyes, who was old enough to understand who had done it, but not capable enough to understand why. I had ripped out pages of my story about previous abuse. But as the blood ran from my nose, past my mouth, and fell onto the floor, it became a carbon copy. It bled through and revealed what was written on those missing pages. The repetition of it caused twice as much pain.

Sunday mornings were always hard. A normal wakeup call was me standing over him with a hot steaming plate of food. Bacon, sausage, eggs, and grits. His usual. Cooking used to be a way to show him that I loved him. It reminded me of watching my grandmother. She would open my grandfather's pop and slowly pour it into the glass. Afterwards they'd flirt as she took his plate away. I wanted to have a marriage like theirs, but soon everything felt like grievous marital duties. He got to sleep in late while I ran around getting everyone ready. "It's time to get up," I said empty-handedly. Then I went downstairs to put a load of clothes in the washing machine.

Suddenly, I was interrupted by the thunderous sound of footsteps. I stood speechless as he yelled, "What is your problem?" I couldn't understand what had just happened. I felt like I'd awaken a raging giant. I found myself being dragged backwards by his forceful advance. I moved further and further back, stumbling until finally he slammed me on the couch. I fell back and found myself awkwardly pinned down like prey. His body crushed me as his forearm was held firmly across my face.

"Get off of me!" I heaved searching for leverage, so that I could wiggle from underneath the fallen tree. I exhausted all my strength trying to push up using both hands, then I felt his hand wedged between mine. He took my pointer and middle fingers in his enormous grasp. A cry for mercy beamed from my eyes like a blinding light, but it was extinguished by his blank stare. Then, a gut-wrenching scream left my mouth and hit the walls like a ball bouncing back and forth without direction. I felt a crack and looked down to find my middle finger deformed and violently torn out of socket. I kicked him in the chest to break free, but I fainted in his arms as he pulled and popped it back into place.

The triage nurse glanced over my shoulder periodically as she examined me. My finger wasn't the real problem. The look in her eyes said she doubted my answer when she asked if I felt safe at home. Again, I had been tracked down and cornered by the beast. He warned that if I told the truth, he would show them the bruise on his chest from the kick. He made me feel like I would never be believed. Somehow someone would misinterpret what happened and I would be blamed again.

(status update)

Great pain equals GREATNESS!

I thought about the reason I'd come to the house. I was there to get rid of the pain. I turned on one of my son's favorite videos and held him closely waiting for him to fall asleep. He was a brave soldier fighting off the enemy of sleep. He slowly scooted down the plush mattress. He planted his feet, took his stance, and refused to be rocked. Something in him knew that if he took his eyes off of me, I'd be gone. Gone downstairs to the closed garage where I'd turn on the car. Hoping I'd start to drift off and the hurtful memories with me. I wanted to feel my first moment of peace. Finally, the lateness of the hour defeated the valiant soldier. The watchful guard fell asleep standing up. His back pressed against the edge of the bed. Carefully, I lay him down. I looked at him and started to say my silent goodbyes, but he woke up frantically. He reached out for me. Something in his touch screamed, "Mommy don't leave me!"

I picked up the phone and dialed. "What is it about me? Why did you beat me? Each word emptied my lungs and vibrated throughout my body like my last. I knew the call must have taken him by surprise. Our daughter, who is sixteen, was a baby when we split. I didn't know what he was thinking, or what type of answer to expect. We barely spoke since both of us had gotten married to someone else. Would he say get over it? I watched him holiday after holiday coming to the house to pick up my daughter's overnight bag. Over and over again his feet left the porch.

I continued to breathe heavily. The shaky desperation of my voice must have registered on the

Richter scale of his heart. I waited quietly as the tears poured down my face like water crashing against a wall. Finally, he answered. "I did it, because I wasn't a man. I was trying to make you respect me by force instead of earning it. I should have never hit you," he said regretfully. It fit. The final piece of the puzzle popped into place. Those words strengthened me. I started to reclaim myself, as I moved on and rid myself of him.

My Way of Escape

I don't believe it,

Me a bubble,

Drifting gently over the sun-lit city.

It was a beautiful site.

The smell of mayflowers is so pretty and sweet.

As I peer into the sky,

I see clouds momentarily floating to a new place,

It is their resting bed.

High in the sky, such as I,

Floating with the breezes of the wind,

On a wind of a song,

Letting the melody take me home.

The freedom of the wind let me look at myself.

Who am I?

Why am I me?

Let love and peace float in my heart, and the wind inside me,

For freedom is what I thrive for.

Pre- Eulogy

I don't want to be dead to be heard.
Even though I have this vision of a classroom of poets
dissecting my piece,
After I'm deceased.

Why can't my words be heard now,
In the middle of my metamorphosis,
When I'm changing from one thing to another,
When the lessons are fresh and more profound,
Why can't my words have more weight,
When I'm made to wait,
On being great.

Before the national recognition,
When I'm just a black girl with a pen,
Who doesn't have a man, and lost lots of friends.

When I'm looked at as just a starving artist,
Who does gigs for free,

Before the contracts and the attention,

When no one knows me, and they can't see,

The vision,

That is right there, if you stare.

It is etched in stone like the 10 commandment's tablets,

It is unrolled like a scroll from the Dead Sea,

But no one knows,

Because it's me.

Dreams

My dreams,

Have dreams.

Vivid, detailed dreams,

That keep me awake,

More than I actually sleep.

Planning,

Thinking,

Accepting in my heart,

That a dream this deep,

Has to be a reality.

It is the truth.

Not just true to me.

The Flower and the Bee   (Fable)

I'm tired of being surrounded by loneliness. To others, it appears I'm embraced by a populated field of sun gold daisies. To me, it is a maze of isolation, a monotonous repetition that chokes out my individuality like a weed. In silence, I sit watching the honeycomb sway in the breeze, pulsating with life, and humming sweet melodies. I imagine being invited to join them for the elegant affair. Surrounded by golden honey like fine china and freshly buffed silverware. Eagerly waiting at the table for the Queen to enter the room where she'll be greeted by smiles and curtseys.

I'm snapped back from my wonderful daydream by Bee's prickly placed feet on my petals. In dread, I'm forced to open my legs and allow his invasive advance. He breathes deeply to rob me of my sweet savor. He prods around my body without permission. His stamina strong continuously going around my stamen until he makes my leaves shake. Then he takes from me. Mission accomplished. Leaving me in utter disgust. Feeling his deep thrust. I'm left with not even the small satisfaction of running my hands across his fury body. I am always used and abandoned. Intrusively approached and then discarded by multiple transactions that leave me empty and drained. I don't understand my plight. My path in this life feels more like death every time I'm left with nothing left.

Then one day, I watched as bee again left suddenly. He struggled to remain afloat. On his hind legs were sacs of golden flakes, and his fury body was drenched in it. No wonder I couldn't touch him. I stopped my mourning long enough to see him GPS through 100's of flowers. Turning left, then right, and left again mile after mile. I realized that field of flowers were full of my children. My anthers had proudly released in response to the Bee's climatic buzzing. Like a doctor, Bee had artificially inseminated as he traveled from the male part of me to the female part of each flower. All this time, I'd been disconnected from this beautiful field of daisies not knowing they belonged to me.

 I watched in the distance as Bee arrived back to the honeycomb. There the household bees helped him unpack my pollen filled load like putting away groceries after a trip to the store. It was then that I realized my plight was for a purpose. My path in this life a flower filled path. I found myself part of the 5 million flowers it takes to make just one pint of honey. The honeycomb wasn't rejoicing over the Queen bee. It was swaying in the breeze, pulsating with life, humming sweet melodies as the scout bee waggles inside it. Revealing his secret directions that would lead back to me.

Poetry is Like...

I love what I do.

It's like wanting to fly and being given wings.

Loving music and being gifted to sing.

Having perfect pitch,

Able to harmonize quickly.

Never being trained and finding out you are a prodigy.

It is like never being able to hear, and having

something open your ears,

To babies cooing, ocean waves, and birds chirping,

It is like being given a remedy for pain,

To years worth of hurting.

It is like a baby being frustrated, because she can't

express what she wants

        vs.

Writing so beautifully on paper that when spoken,

You can see the bold letters and feel the creative

fonts.

It is poetry.

A way to get to what is inside of me.

Turn Pages into Palettes

Colorful words,

Earth tones turned into reds, yellow, and oranges,

Exploding with vibrance.

I need my words to vibrate off of the page,

Living words,

Words of comfort,

Uplifting,

Bearing your burden words,

Full of spirit that you feel instead of read,

Words raised from the page more profound than braille,

I need the ink on the pages that I write on,

To stain your fingers,

Cause fingerprints all over the page,

Reveal a blueprint for what is deep inside of you.

I need my words to leave a residue.

I want to erase every negative word,

Every insecurity every "I can't" feeling,

Create a powerful perseverance,

Acknowledgement of self

Yourself,

The "I can do anything" self.

The "I am enough" self,

The "world is waiting to hear from me" self.

Allows you to dream.

Together we will travel into a dream state,

Purple hues, blues: sky blues, blues that are barely there,

Turquoise, blue greens, jumping all over the spectrum,

Darkness to light,

Experiencing each almost physically.

Allowing ourselves to soak in the prisms of color and light,

Healing,

Feeling the intangible as we become untangled,

From the unmanageable.

Allowing ourselves to be free-

Mixing, experimenting, creating,

What we need on our beautiful canvas.

Invading the whiteness and blankness,

Creating on nothingness,

Something exquisite and profound.

I created words to help you create art.

A representation of sentences, fragments,

Similes and metaphors,

Concrete to abstract art,

Thrive and vibe artist!

Stroke your brush as I caress pen to pad,

Let the muse cause you to open up,

Your extremities and go deep,

Penetrate, escalate,

Move rhythmically,

Pour unto your canvas until it reveals

What your mind creates.

Bring the canvas,

Into submission of your hands,

Manipulating up and down,

Back and forth,

Circular motions,

Create and do with it as you will.

Landscape at Dawn

Before dawn faint chirping,

In the darkness, beauty becomes memories.

Each night, the birds encourage themselves,

While planning for morning.

The light sends darkness into a slow-retreat,

The heavens break.

Each morning, the birds rejoice as they bathe in the sunlight.

At night, what made the birds chirp,

Without seeing the sun creep over the horizon?

The answer;

Also, makes us believe.

In Honor of my Mother   (Prose)

It's the first beautiful day of spring and the fisherman begin to take their seat along the banks in first row orchestra formation. The lake is played like a harp from all the fishing line being cast and retrieved in the deep as the zing and plops play sweet melodies. The minnows and night crawlers that are hooked on the line listen to this classical concerto as they are made to wait for their demise. The birds provide the signal from the conductor to play faster during the next movement as motorboats begin to troll the river with bait hanging off the back of the boat. The snagging of fish out the water is nothing more than the conductor's baton moved swiftly upwards to pick up the pace of the melody. Opening and closing of tackle boxes provide the consistent beat from the bass drums, and all the lures provide the tinkling of the cymbals.

Meanwhile, this outdoor concert gets applauds, along with a standing ovation from the sun. I've never seen a real orchestra that wasn't played on Norris Lake. The lake being the orchestra pit, and the mountains sit in the seats of the theater listening attentively with me.

Aunt Stella   (Short Story)

Helping Aunt Stella with the quilts was the only way we communicated. The room was full of game show noises and screams from the next contestant walking down to play, but between us there was complete silence. She would hand me the cardboard cutout. It was used to cut fabric into whatever quilt she was working on next: wedding rings, Dutch girls, star quilts, diamond patchwork, and square patchwork. If she looked up while I was cutting, that meant I didn't move the cardboard close enough to the edge, and I was wasting too much fabric. If she started to shift in her chair toward another pile of colored fabrics, that meant that I was giving her too much of the same colored pieces. I needed to switch it up a bit. The only time she really spoke was when lunch time was nearing. She deciphered the smells that were in the air as she explained the menu. All day long, I imagined what it would be as I cut patterns, bending over slightly, so that she couldn't hear my stomach growling. She had tried to teach me how to sew, but between my huge knots, pulling the thread too hard and breaking it, and not being able to stitch in a straight line, Aunt Stella finally decided, my job was cutting the fabric. I loved cutting the fabric.

    Years later, I walked into Aunt Stella's house. I had grown up so much that I no longer wanted to sift through bags of fabrics, but I started to miss the time we spent together. As soon as I came through the door and walked past the kitchen she said, "Have some cake, baby." I doubled back to go into the kitchen, and I looked everywhere, but there was no cake to be found. Instead there were a few roaches that scattered across the countertop, which is definitely something I had never seen there before. As I came out of the kitchen my eyes were met by my mother's tearful death stare, and I knew not to open my mouth. The house was run down now, everything grossly out of place. The room smelled of urine and feces. Aunt Stella's gown was stained. That was the first time I saw her wig cocked sideways or backwards, I'm not sure which. We ended up moving her into a nursing home. That was the summer I learned about Alzheimer's. I had heard Aunt Stella tell so many stories I lost count. Stories of grocery store trips, men in the trees watching her, elaborate meals she spent all day cooking. Only to realize the pieces of patchwork could no longer be sown together. Her memories were now a quilt unfinished.

Mom's Hands

She has her hands,

Time blurred the strongly defined lines,

Losing them in between the folds of wrinkly skin,

Snake- like patterns now replace what was once as smooth as a baby's behind.

Perfect, elongated fingers,

Slightly bent showing years of use.

Hands just like her mother's hands.

Long beautifully manicured nails,

Her real nails,

The only remarkable thing left intact was strong,

Long, real, beautifully manicured nails,

Not covered in acrylic,

Hard only on the surface,

Yet thinning and dying underneath.

Looking at her hands,

Which were her mother's hands, made her cry.

Neither one of us was strong enough to hold her hand

as she died.

Our hearts broke as we heard the gurgling,

Her breath so shallow like we were watching,

Her heart stop beating.

Her hands folded back into a fetal position,

Telling us death was near.

We left before her spirit left,

So that we could rest,

Remembering her alive,

Not dying in our arms.

Chosen for the Fire

Many are called, but few are chosen.
To be chosen, you must endure sufferings.
Come face to face with fear, even the shadow of death,
Yet see the peace that only God's word can bring.

Some have been chosen for the flood,
God says those that sow in tears reap in joy.
Do you know God accepts those who are afflicted?
For that is when he speaks, "That's my girl, or my boy."

Surely, the waters cannot overtake thee!
In this you must believe.
You have been chosen by the Master,
Even the devil stands in awe of what he sees.

I have been chosen for the fire,

Through sickness and pain, I am purified,

Now I can grab hold of the vision,

It is me, and my family, who are led safely to the other side.

I've gone through the fire,

However, I am not burned.

Although I still remember seeing the ashes

fall all around me,

What an awesome lesson I have learned.

Our lack of faith fights against the word that is in us.

Sometimes we fail to realize, it is true and sure.

Our trails are designed to give us brand new revelation,

To what we have been called and chosen to endure.

Midnight

I wore a two-piece bathing suit,

With a tiny blue sailboat on the left breast.

I hate that I remember the rest.

I didn't swim that day.

I wore the bathing suit to play,

Barefoot in the rain.

I ignored their three faces,

Pressed against the windowpane.

They watched me as I bent over on the sidewalk,

Taking a stick to stir mud pies.

I was innocent,

But now I know,

There was a heinous look in their eyes.

I sang songs from the Wizard of Oz,

While singing, "Follow the Yellow Brick Road."

In an instant,

I was pulled into their garage,

Having them tearing at my clothes.

Three brothers,

One almost in high school,

Two not far behind,

With intentions of raping me,

A little girl,

Only 9.

It was midnight in the garage,

I could barely see a thing,

But blindly,

With everything I had,

I started to kick and swing.

I don't understand,

How I got away,

-------- My virginity intact,

But sadly,

Something else,

Was taken,

That to this day,

I still want back.

My Near Miss

I hate to be almost raped.

To have his eyes penetrate my skin with wicked fantasies,

Projected through me like I'm film,

Playing through a projector movie.

I was once invisible.

Just an innocent child able to play all day,

Until he looked my way.

My skin now crawling,

My curves appalling,

In his mind, I'm ripe and ready for the picking.

But my roots haven't grown deep enough,

They haven't sucked up enough of the soil's nutrients.

Yes, I've blossomed some, but I don't even have strength to fully bloom.

I'm not able to stand in front of a mirror and like what I see,

Yet, already, he has made me filthy.

Already, his mental maneuvers,

The way his lustfulness hovers over me,

Has oppressed me.

I'm searching to cover up,

While he is undressing me.

I'm covering up with shame, with weight gain,

Dressing too old for my age,

Because self- blame made me ask myself how I misbehaved.

What did I do to deserve the stares?

I've been told to talk.

To tell if anyone has touched me,

But how do I explain this feeling of violation,

That tore holes in my flesh without penetration.

That makes me feel self-conscious even to this day,

Not ever knowing those first feelings of being looked at as pretty,

Never being admired,

Only desired.

Not having time to learn to love self,

Before my self-esteem was perverted by someone else.

What I Should Not Say

My great grandma's world was so different than theirs.
She thought granddaddy was so protective of his little angels.
She never even questioned,
Why did he sleep with the girls, and make her sleep with the boys?

When she pats her knee and grins about what a good man he was, she can't see the disapproving looks.
As she reminisces – Their lips are closed tight.

They still smell his penis,
Even though he is dead, and they are grown with children and grandchildren of their own.
I blame her for remembering a husband that loved her,
While they remember a daddy they want to forget.

Stone

(Dedicated to someone, I will keep anonymous,
who suffered abuse on 4/26/18).

You are not the stones,
Near someone's fishing hole,
Where millions of beers have overturned,
And spilled,
Where bait has been balanced,
Catfish, bluegills,
Have been killed,
Reeling them in one at a time,
No,
You are not that kind.

You are not the stones that skip over the pond,
Whirled from the hands,
Of the scrawny, little brown-haired boy,
Or the stones that have been used for toys,

A replacement for missing jacks,

No,

You are worth,

More than that.

You are not the stones,

That are near the gravel pit.

Where steel-toed workers "haucked" and spit,

So, let me explain it.

You are a precious stone,

A ruby,

A gem,

Even though you were treated,

As nothing by him.

You are not to be degraded,

Called out of your name,

Fat-shamed,

Not to be on the receiving end,

When he shifts the blame.

Not to be called stupid,

Emotional, insecure,

A whore, A THOT,

You are a queen!

And you…You will not!

Punch her,

Smack her or kick her.

I flow in the power of God,

To uplift and equip her,

To know,

She is a ---

Rare,

Precious,

Stone.

Choice

I had my "pro-choice", choice

Taken away.

Pregnant at 13,

Due on my 14th birthday.

How did I end up,

Legs in stirrups,

Giving birth to a child,

I wouldn't take home.

Not aborting ......

This wasn't a fetus without a heartbeat,

I had already felt this baby kick,

I had carried it month after month,

......................Almost six.

It all started with a phone call from Planned Parenthood,

Her voice sounding like a sweet grandmother,

But her tone....

Warned,

It wouldn't be good.

She explained how much of a disgrace and embarrassment I was,

How this child shouldn't have to pay for my sin,

That an appointment was made,

So I had to come in.

During the ultrasound the tech asked if I wanted to know the sex,

I turned and just looked around the room,

Surely, I'm too far along for an abortion,

She thought,

But she assumed.

Money can get rid of any situation,

"No, I don't want to know,"

I whispered, in

Complete devastation.

I went back home to take pills,

Before coming in the next day,

I laid on the couch----

Moaning, rocking in pain,

A pain that I felt,

Would never go away.

The next day I was terrified,

As the doctor approached the table,

I tried to hold back the tears,

But I just wasn't able.

I screamed, I cried,

My nails cut the nurse's wrist,

The doctor grit his teeth and said,

"Bitch, you weren't crying when you were getting it,

So don't cry during this."

I was a child stripped of a choice,

That was so precious to me.

Partial-birth abortion,

Is not the "pro-choice"

Face that you see.

It is a secret, back dealing,

Whisper behind closed doors,

That makes young rape victims,

Feel like whores.

Safehouse

The worst thing in life,

Is a functioning addict.

My mother's ability to cope,

Left her without culpability,

She wanted me to ignore,

What she was doing,

But her addiction was real to me.

I learned quickly,

An orphan isn't an orphan,

Because they don't have a home,

An orphan is an orphan,

Because they are alone!

I was disciplined by phone,

Welcomed home by latchkey,

Told my mother was always working,

That was only-- PARTLY ---TRUE.

Her job held her captive,

To pay for her addiction,

In my mind,

She had been kidnapped,

She was missing!

My cries for attention,

Were never listened to.

What is a home?

What is a safehouse,

Without you!

Mayonnaise

With a horrified look in her eyes,

She said she HATED mayonnaise.

It reminded her of thick, creamy,

Ejaculations that she could feel,

And taste.

Walking away,

Wiping the stickiness off her face.

I was left carrying,

The pain of a friend.

As she died never confessing who,

And he lived,

TEMPORARILY not paying for that sin.

Pain

Hurting others, causing them to push away.

Pain wakes the spirit of abandonment.

Pain welcomes it as a beggar would welcome an injury,

A broken leg,

A broken arm,

Anything to gain them greater sympathy.

Pain is a wickedness that feeds on being brokenhearted-

The sting of it.

The burn.

The breathless agony.

Refusing to be comforted,

Pain fears to be healed.

It is full of complaints and constant dissatisfaction,

Overflowing from twisted lips.

Frowns that frown.

Suspicious looks at those you should trust.

Disapproving everything others enjoy.

Hurt is normal.

Enjoyment-

A discomforting abstract.

You are uncomfortable having a heart,

That does not throb and ache in pain.

Wounded Soldier

Lord my heart has been broken.
In the fire I've been tried.
I need to find a hiding place,
Deliver me from the hurt,
Draw me closer to your bleeding side.

Let me feel the hem of your garment brush against me,
That I may receive your healing virtue.
Pour oil in my wounds,
Encourage my soul,
So that I can make it through.

Take away the hurtful things that people have said.
Both in the world and in the church,
Comfort me like a father does his child.
Help me forget the tears that I have shed,
Flowing from a heart,

Broken and reviled.

Teach me how to have so many against me,
But still keep a smile on my face,
Hold me close, and lift up my head,
Show me how to draw from this well,
Even though I'm surrounded by a barren, desert place.

Take me into your presence.
I need to go even further that I've ever gone before.
Other times, I've gone just to draw strength for the fight,
But this time, I'm a wounded soldier,
Returning from war.

Surprise Ending

I loved differently than I had been loved,

Differently than she had been loved,

Trying to break a generation curse.

Nothing's worse,

"I love you" was never meant to be silent.

I spoke a language I was never taught,

The love language of time.

Refusing to buy my way out of being absent,

I didn't want to leave another heart in fragments,

I needed them to know I was there.

I chose eleven years of celibacy,

Not just to honor God,

I didn't trust myself to decide,

Didn't want them to ever see my heart broken, or

tears fall from my eyes,

I knew love wasn't that trustworthy.

I thought I made all the right moves,

Had cracked the code,

Done better than my family had ever done before,

Only to stand toe to toe with my daughter as she calls me a whore,

Being a parent is hard.

Not Just A Mother

You are not just a mother,

Celebrated for one simple role.

……………………You are so complex.

Always giving more,

Than what others expect.

You are to be decoded for hidden meanings,

Like the videos we watch,

Or the songs we sing.

To sum it all up,

My sister,

You are everything!

You are gifted, creative, ambitious,

Educated with,

Common sense,

Book smarts, and

Being up on game.

You excel and walk with pride,

Because of,

Not Despite of,

............The things you overcame.

You are who you are,

Even when you are too pissed,

To act like a lady.

Too much in love,

To think like a man.

In fact,

Who can hang on, give up,

Start over,

Bounce back,

Better than we can?

Who else is able to turn failures,

Into an "Oprah", "Harpo",

"Own", "O' That's so Good",

Type of brand?
You aren't just great when there is a "Who Runs the World, Girls" anthem,
Or a "Black Girls Rock" hashtag.
You slay,
Even in a no name outfit,
With a knock off handbag.

So what,
Your hair and nails aren't always on fleek.
You know how to twist it up,
Switch it up, and
Make it unique.

You congratulate and clap for others,
Who don't appreciate you.
Who wait for you,
To say something,
So they can clap back.

Then you show up... still smiling,

Like your character isn't being attacked.

You are a mother,

But that one word will never define,

Someone who is so truly,

Phenomenal, and

Awesome by design.

The Chameleon

Life is plans adjusted,

Changed and amended.

Concrete promises that appear

-Open ended-

Life assigns pain,

To the undeserving,

Who pray to be relieved.

While some mock God,

Others struggle to believe.

Our hearts and minds,

Hate and forgive,

Without comprehension.

Being sure of life,

Yet facing circumstances,

That make you feel apprehension.

Everything I have observed says,

"Life is so misleading."

Yet we strive to live,

Keep believing,

Dreaming,

Waiting on dreams to be fulfilled.

While everything changes,

Nothing is as it appears.

The End

Have you ever had to slam on the brakes?
Not realizing that traffic stopped up ahead.
You desperately hope you have enough time to stop.
Your heart pounds,
You end up veering to the left or right,
Hoping to avoid a possible crash up ahead.

I feel that way about life.
We are always caught off guard by unexpected circumstances,
Always surprised that our smooth journey is met with an unexpected, abrupt halt.

We have no idea what's up ahead.
What test results will alter our lives forever.

We just desperately hope that we have enough time to stop.
Enough time to stop being fearful and pursue our dreams.
Enough time to quit making excuses,

Quit procrastinating and just get things accomplished.

Your heart pounds when you think,

About the possible failures you could run into,

Not even realizing that not trying, not doing-

Is the ONLY failure in life.

We veer to the left:

Getting too emotional, allowing bitterness to set in,

Ending up being cynical and mad at the world.

We veer to the right:

Becoming more settled and temperate in our actions,

Finding our faith, grounding, and footing,

Learning to walk in our purpose.

We hope to avoid the crash up ahead,

Dying prematurely,

Dying before leaving our mark,

Dying before exhausting ourselves with helping

others, encouraging others,

Giving to others as we give ourselves up to this life,

Finally, finishing our work, so that we deserve to close

our eyes and rest.

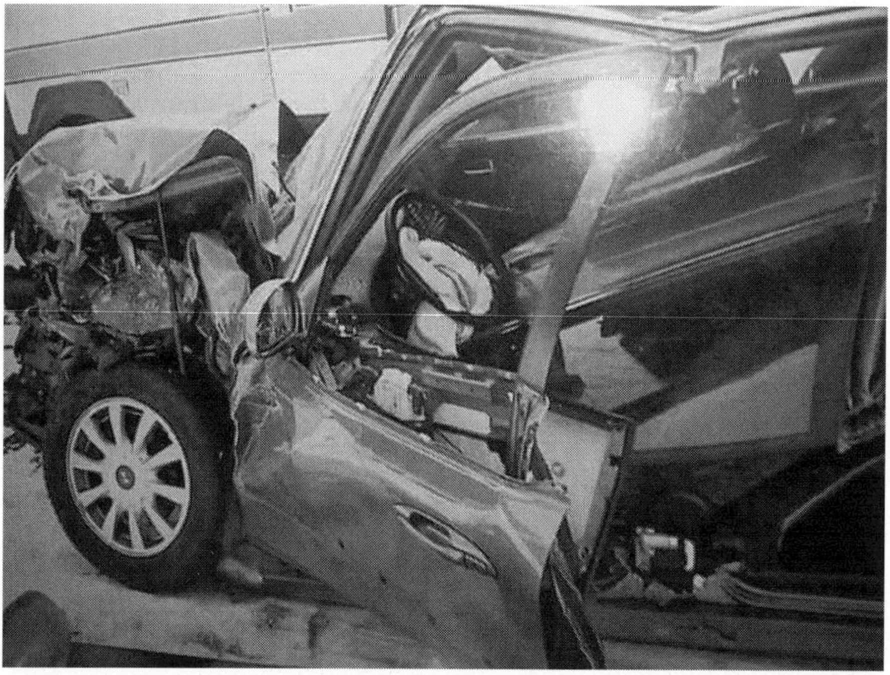

What is Beautiful

What's beautiful is seeing a tear-

Fall from another woman's cheek,

Feeling the lump in my throat,

The burning in my chest,

Sharing the pain of her story,

As she begins to share.

Experiencing it, as if I was there.

The beauty of helping someone heal,

Helping pick up the shards of glass,

From each other's brokenness,

While being willing to be cut again.

Learning what it takes to help hearts mend.

Come Back Up   (Short Story)

I didn't want to be the stereotypical black girl who couldn't swim. I remember getting my mom's permission to take swimming classes at the Boys and Girls Club downtown. I was eager to show off my new bathing suit that day. I remember the male instructor, tall and slender. He must have been very tall, because somehow the description of what his face looked like got lost in the clouds, while everything else: deep voice, chest covered with a t-shirt, red and blue swimming trunks, and white gym shoes are vividly remembered. As he pulled off his gym shoes, he directed all of us, ages 10-16, to line up in order of our birth months. We all scrambled around shouting out,

" November, February, June, and May," pushing each other aside, pulling each other forward until we were in month order. I was one of the last ones to be placed in line, because, as soon as he said month order, my birthday month, March, caused me to feel paralyzed.

"Now jump off the diving board into the 12 foot," was the only instructions he spoke. My mind totally blacked out. I don't remember the other children going in, or coming to the top. I don't remember any sounds of children talking, playing, or cheering. The only thing I remember is feeling water rush past me on my left and right, as my hands were spread open wide. I sank to the bottom at lightening speeds where I sat there Indian style, jaws full of air, heart full of fear, knowing soon the air would be gone, and I'd have to take in a mouthful of water. The instructor must have finally realized I was buried underneath those 12 feet of water a bit too long, and decided he had to jump in and rescue me.

When we reached the top, he scolded, "Why didn't you come back up to the top? You were supposed to push off the bottom, swim towards the light, and come back up." Funny thing is where were those instructions before I jumped off the diving board? Somehow that experience seems symbolic of my life. My need to try things out of the desire not to fit into various stereotypes. The harsh reality that more than likely I'll have to jump right in, sink to the bottom, be scolded for not knowing what to do even though all the valuable information to help me rise to the top will be excluded: push off the bottom, swim towards the light, and come back up.

Eradication of Ventriloquy

(A work inspired by "The Freedman" sculptor, 1863, by John Quincy Adams.)

I want you to speak about your perfectly sculpted back,

How smooth-

A back void of engraved evidence,

Left behind from masters' whip.

I need you to speak about your pedicured feet,

Feet that should show how you shuffled,

Across miles of weary ground,

Searching for freedom-

Trying to sniff it out like a hungry bloodhound.

Please speak about your calloused hands,

Hands that sifted through soft white cotton,

Presented as strong, free hands,

Instead of hands deflated by the cruel puncture marks of thorns.

Speak about the woman you could not protect,

The child that was torn from her arms,

Your woman.

Your child.

Your heart that said they were still yours,

Even as you watched them leave with the man that

held the bill of sale.

Say what the sculptor's hands smoothed over,

Reveal how he attempted to remove past truths.

How degrading to set a man free and deny him

equality.

How sad to silence by omission.

He silenced you-

Sculpted in bronze,

Displaying you as "The Freedman."

"I, Too, am America 2019"
(Inspired by "I, Too" Langston Hughes, 1925)

I swim in swimming pools.

I don't have to be beaten and run off,

That's last half a century's rules.

I don't have to be stopped at the gated community,

Asked to see my keys,

Asked where am I going,

As if I can't afford the rent,

Or they'd never give a house to me,

I, too, am America.

Since when were restaurants "re- segregated,"

Now I have to debate, is it safe,

Just drinking coffee before ordering my plate,

While I'm waiting on friends who are running late.

Will they call the police?

Will they make me leave?

Are they waiting on an excuse to take my freedom

back from me,

I, too, am America.

My sons and daughters aren't a threat,

Running around like rabbit dogs,

They aren't deer in a field during deer hunting season,

You don't have to pursue them,

Then shoot them,

Claiming fear for your life was the reason,

I, too, am America.

I'll go to sleep tonight covered in the Constitution,

Curled up reading my Emancipation Proclamation,

Wondering when something will be written,

That will make me part of this nation.

I, too, am America.

Harlem

Hey Harlem,

You are part of me like you are my ancestry,

You are like a father who left me,

But I found you,

You call to me through jazz songs and blues,

You've been my muse,

My Langston Hughes,

My old school,

That's still relevant,

With messages that are prevalent,

A meter and cadence that I can feel,

Dope lines that are real,

You spit for me,

With the same passion that is heard in a slam,

I'd marry you,

If you'd ask for my hand.

A Black Woman in Corporate America

I had to face racism.
Every moment in the face of racism is a pivotal, defining moment.
Corporate America takes what is defined as truth and the norm to us,
Bends and distorts that truth,
Until it is shaped into a lie.
The lie I was told was, "If people know that you are a black woman, even if they don't say it to you, they will think to themselves, that you are a dumb broad."
A Black woman, not unprofessional, not so- called "ghetto", not inarticulate, not that I'm not knowledgeable, just that I'm black.
If fact, I was knowledgeable enough to clarify all that before those words began to fuel anger inside of me. Anger due to that ignorance and hypocrisy. Anger that I brought excellence into a company that was merely mediocrity, but they still hated me, because I'm black.
I was left to unravel hatred's lie.

The truth behind the lie is that I was despised for my worth.
Even though the company was now worth more because of me,
Even though they said good mornings there was envy,
Envy, because sadly they had never seen a black woman like me.
Since I couldn't be seen collecting multi-million dollar accounts by phone,
The racist attack was based on how my voice sounds over the phone,
Attacked by saying I "sound black".
What's wrong with black? Isn't it just a skin tone?
What's wrong is that someone would judge on that alone.

I Don't Want to be Black

I don't want to be black,
Those are the words that my ten year old son told me with tears in his eyes.
He is tired of being viewed as a threat.
5'1", 130 pounds, broad shoulders-
Easily mistaken for a man,
A man who is black,
Another black man, who could easily be shot in the back.

Seen as having a weapon,
Even when he is empty-handed.
Seen as resisting arrest,
Because he doesn't understand why he is arrested.
Seen as obstructing when what is obstructed is his liberty,
Not wanting to be black,

Because there's too many things he is taught not to be.

Not wanting to be black,
Even though his black role models are hard-working,
Educated examples of who to be.
Not wanting to be black,
Because it's hard to be black, and feel free.

Warned that when in the presence of police don't move,
Don't turn, never run,
Don't grab or hold onto anything,
That they can say is a gun.

Warned son please, "Watch who you hang with".
What is seen is not always what is perceived.
Warned over and over,
So I won't be the next-
Black mother left to grieve.

Told to never become irate,

Even if he is falsely blamed or accused.

That " Hands up, don't shoot!"

Really means don't move!

Because " I was in fear for my life,"

Is the excuse they will use,

And even when there is evidence,

That is not the truth,

Justice is refused.

February

There is a reason why his----story being taught,
In history is no longer working for me.
The reason used to be,
Everyone who had done anything weren't my
Color.

Black inventor's ideas stolen,
Buried under patents.
The success of those inventions a mockery,
Like white men in black face.
Yet there's no remorse, or feelings of disgrace.

Traditions outlawed, culture stripped, and black
Influence denied.
Robbed from a wealth of African richness,
Given-
Assumed by another who hates black pride.
Omission= the greatest lie of all times.

So history (his--- story) has never been a real
interest of mine.

Today, I hate history, because the present-
Even more insane, 40-50 years later,
I'm still called out of my name.
"Coon, Enee-grow" printed on jerseys,
No different than spitting out "Nigger" as they
Stood so close they stepped on toes,
Captured and beaten down by fists,
Or the powerful water let loose from the hose.

Telling "My" son that he would be lynched if he
Wouldn't stay on task and be still,
No different from using the Holy Bible to say
My son and I are inferior, because it is
God's will.

Having lawmakers and public figures that

Degrade, assault, and harass women,

No different than slave masters raping slaves

As if they were entitled,

So entitled,

Is this how history is made?

Is this our thanks for building the country we

Were never welcomed in,

Is this how we are repaid?

We've given a racist president a mic and a

Tweet,

International race relations,

Our own nation's relations,

Which already struggled to stand-

Has fallen in defeat.

Well history,

The history we are making today.

You are so immoral, hateful, and unjust!

We know the real truth,

His---- story, you believe what you must.

No Longer Winning

Headwrap,
My bandage from mental attacks,
From what others thought of me.
I had to have a lobotomy,
Just to think clearly.
But the Word says,
Let this mind be in you,
That was also in me,
So in essence,
Your negativity,
Fulfilled destiny!
My healing,
Brings greatness,
Through mind framing,
I've been elevated,
To places,
Run faster,
Than others,
In the same race,
Not to win,
In this case,
But as a testament of his grace.

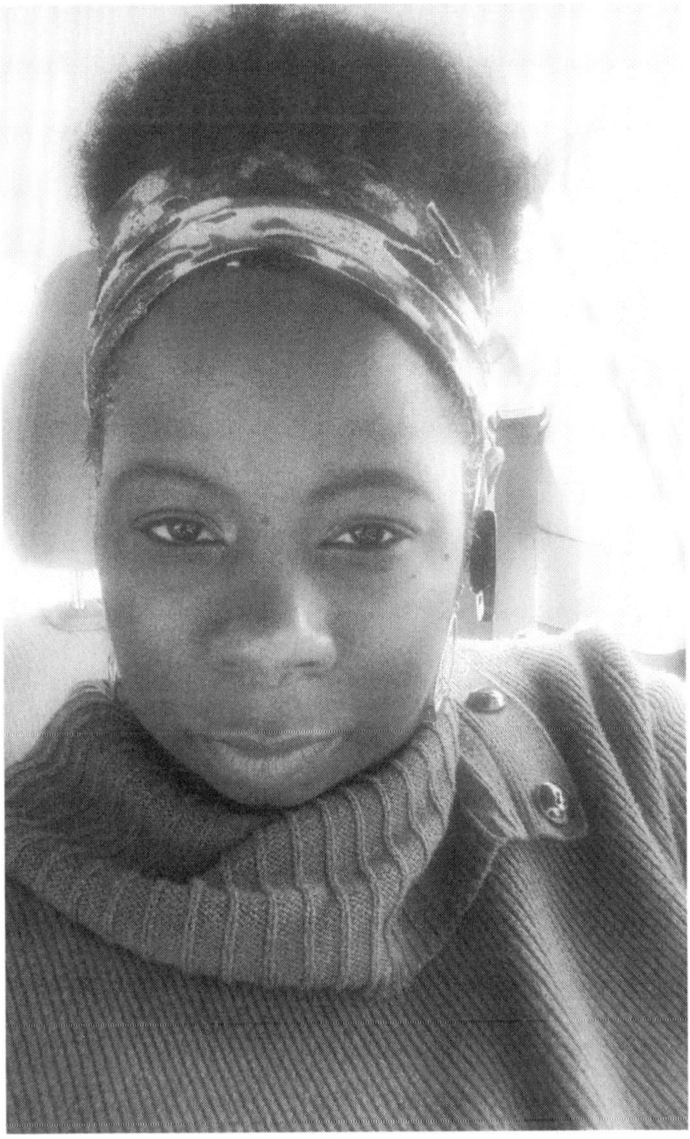

Full and Free

My hips weren't shaped in a one-size, fits-all mold.

Swaying with an "Omphf" rhythm,

Lace doesn't drape or flow,

These hips wear the clothes.

These lips aren't made for quick pecks.

They cause our faces to caress.

My tongue enters like black coffee,

Taking in cream.

Leaving us feeling warm and undressed.

They come all over the page!

These words aren't confined by my femininity.

They are bursting with raw passion,

Innuendos,

Unleashed sexuality.

My expressions aren't capped by adverbs and adjectives,

To only defined,

Acceptable words.

Levees break in my mind.

Unspoken thoughts,

Dammed and held back are finally heard-

Full and free.

Maybe

Maybe, I'm too plus sized,
No maybe, my dream is too big,
My vision is too wide.

So what, there's not enough space between these thighs.
There is wisdom and knowledge,
Gained through things, I've seen with these eyes.

Maybe, I'm just too dark- skinned,
Is it too much melanin?
Does my shine offend,
Oh, but my shine only offends, those who are dark within.

I won't apologize for not being able to turn it off.
I've been burned.
I've had my fire extinguished.
I've paid the cost,

To shine.

Paid the cost to speak my mind.

I have opinions and good suggestions,

That are powerful like an arsenal of weapons.

I am a leader who knows how to follow directions,

And if I'm really led, I can allow him to be the head.

My value does not diminish,

My worth does not fade.

Even though, they say beauty fades, but

I look in the mirror, and I see an endless beauty,

And I say, "That is me."

Now that is the definition of empowering.

Learning to love what others hate.

Realizing what they can't see.

Accepting the beauty on the outside and the inside of me.

Child Proof   (Prose)

In 1967, Dr. Henri Breault (a pediatrician and father) was so upset by the 100,000 annual overdose case that resulted in 100 children dying every year in Canada that he invented a Palm-N-Turn Cap that dropped the child poisoning rates by 91%. However, a Canadian was not the first inventor. In 1986, the University of Texas sent archaeologist to the place now known as Guatemala where they found the first child proof cap was on a vessel left behind by the Mayans. Inside that vessel was chocolate, because the Mayans reverenced and protected chocolate. So much so, it was used in religious ceremonies.

So Dear Black Women:

Dear Chocolate Sisters:

Don't get mad, because someone couldn't get into you. You came in a child proof container. Chocolate comes from a tree that means "food for the Gods." So see not just any man can kiss a Hershey like this. This Ghirardelli had to be handled carefully. Your fondue of brown hue had to be hidden from view. So let him walk out of your life! Let him leave! Because he took one look at you and said, "This Nestle is too much for me."

Public Smile, Private Storm

My real- life story causes people to sit in awkward silence,

So I decided to remain silent.

I have plugged up a mouthful of emotions,

By covering it up with a smile.

Continually saying, "You are happy every day."

Working through my pain,

Angrily, enviously watching others break.

Telling myself, "You are too strong to make that mistake."

Cry at home, alone.

This is a private storm.

Only, I feel the winds shifting,

Letting me know something else is coming.

I watch as the clouds roll in,

While others are busy enjoying the sun.

Meanwhile, over and over,

People say how much they love my smile.

They enjoy the calmness of my presence and my peace,

Yet my heart anxiously breaks into pieces,

Unable to release.

I want to say just hold me, and let me cry,

But all the shoulders I used to cry on are gone.

Some have died.

Others walked away, because they didn't feel needed,

Wasn't sure what they could give me.

Sounds strange,

But that is the life I live.

So much strength, they can't see the pain.

Smiling so brightly, they miss the rain.

Your Right Hand

How could a friendship end that was so dear to me?

I reached out for vapors that disappeared.

Cut deep by disappointment,

My grieving heart asked, "Lord how could you lead me here?"

Sickness my only comfort, I felt cast away,

Ashamed to cry, for in it I travailed.

Mourning for that part of me,

Flooded with feelings I could never tell.

Wanting to give up, but hope would not allow it,

My mind visits the other times you brought me through.

Even if there's no one else I can count on,

Lord, I know I can depend on you.

Here I am looking at the suffering,

Waiting for the glory (in this) to be revealed.

When suddenly, I realize I'm still standing,

It's your right hand that upholds me still.

Introspection

It's hard to look within,

There are so many inconsistencies:

Wearing my feelings on my shoulder,

Having thick skin,

Smile captivating,

Yet broken.

No nonsense,

Shit taking,

To blame,

For most of my pain,

That's why my heart's aching.

Failing to trust some,

Trusting some too much,

Afraid to let someone get close,

Intoxicated by touch.

Always giving,

Sometimes bitter,

Because I gave too much.

Independent,

But wanting a man,

Submissive,

But more than a handful,

I'm 2 hands!!

Everything I love,

Yet can't stand,

Stares me in my face,

And is a part of who I am.

The Butterfly

My beauty,

My purpose,

What I would become,

Was not known when our,

Stars came into line.

We met during an inopportune time.

I was constricted,

Wrapped tightly in my own inhibitions,

Always seeking approval,

Trying to fix it before others,

Looked my way,

No wonder it was easy for other women to

Snatch your attention that way.

I was unattractive,

My beauty held captive,

Trapped in my metamorphosis,

Knowing my life was truly,

More than this.

Struggling to break free internally,

Not knowing that it was building,

Strength in me.

Not knowing that one day,

I'd have beautiful wings,

It was never intended for you to see me fly,

"I" was hidden from view,

"I" wasn't for you.

Imitation

I don't know what is real anymore.

He told me that he loved me.

Not just words....

The type of "telling"....

Where you make someone look into your eyes.

I thought his eyes said I could trust him,

I cleared him with all my family and friends.

He even went to counseling with me,

I know it may sound extreme,

But, in order, for me to introduce him to my son,

To be in the house when the sun came up...

With us...

I had to make sure he was the one.

He said he didn't have a problem with faithfulness.

Even though I told him I'd only been faithful to my ex-husband and him.

He said I could trust him with my heart,

He didn't want to be the reason,

It would be broken again.

He said his children were his life,

But that I was his hope,

I guess that meant a hope for a better life.

He said he didn't want me to be just a girlfriend,

He wanted me to be his partner for life.

I loved him back,

Because my heart was finally convinced,

It was real.

I loved him completely,

Just to find out.

He was denying even being with me.

Now, I'm left to explain,

Instead of sending out wedding invitations,

What I could have sworn was absolutely real,

Was only an imitation.

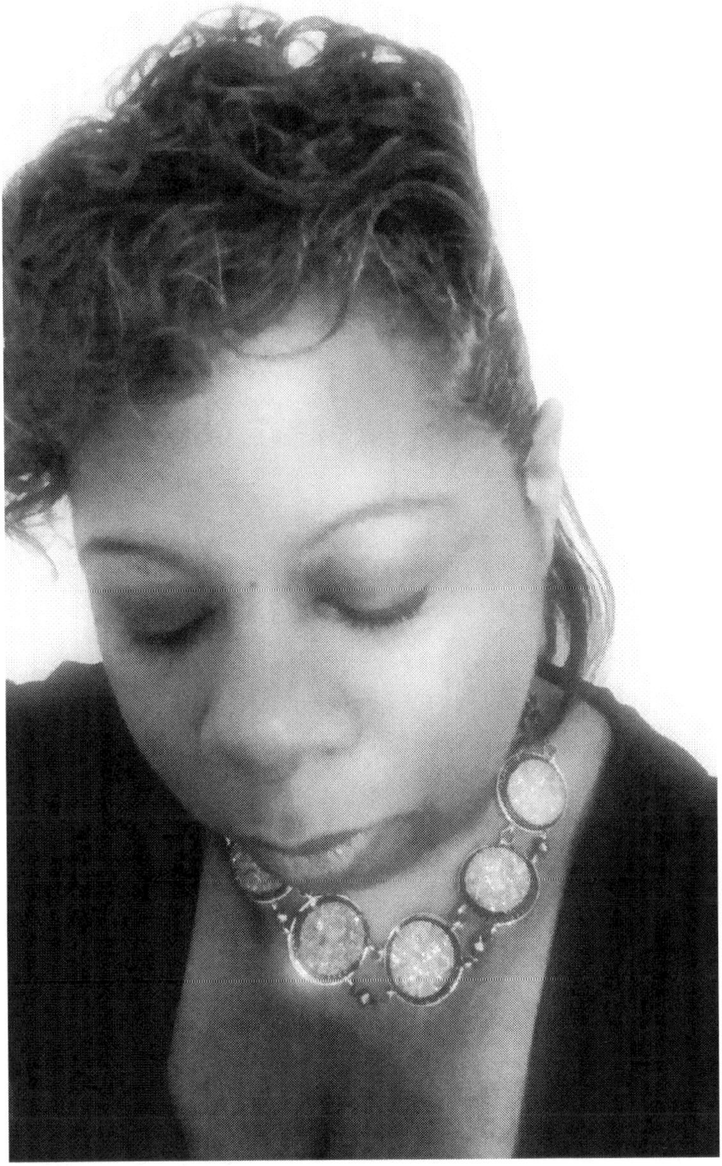

Register

I don't want to wake up on the wrong side of the bed,
Spending my day reassuring myself,
Of things that I already know are true.

I need it to register:
That even though my season, time, and
Opportunity,
Hasn't matched Mr. Right's,
Season, time, and opportunity,
That there is still someone,
Who is right for me.

That some men don't operate in untruths,
They are man enough to stand behind,
What they say and do.

That my beauty doesn't have to compare,
--------------Because it's rare.

That someone will see me and be intrigued,

Enough to say to themselves,

"Hum, what's up?"

That they will sip my chocolate, savoring it,

Yet racing to get to the bottom of my cup,

And I don't mean just in a sexual way.

They will look at me and understand me,

Instead of saying, "She's too deep" and "Why does she over think?"

They will just love me deeply and completely.

My prayers is---------

Please let this register.

Love

Who would dare ask me about love?

I thought I knew love.

I trusted love with all my secrets.

I was an introvert changed,

Into this wonderful person,

Working the room,

Making stunning, witty introductions.

Meeting new people,

Changed my look, my swag.

In full bloom.

Radiant, open,

Giving, and in tune.

Paying attention to what I thought love required.

Intimate with love.

Needing to be naked with love,

Soaking up the skin-to-skin feeling,

The caressing, the touching,

Everything that sex can't give.

Learning to live – in love.

Respecting love,

Letting go of the rolodex of backup plans,

To make this love work,

With only one man.

Only to have love

HURT!

Love made me question,

How I could give so much,

So much, and still

I'm not enough.

Because of love I had to decapitate,

Dismember everything I thought was proof,

That this time it was real.

I had to bury what I feel.

All because of love.

Love for God

So afraid to be alone,
I cried, "Who can give me what I need?"
It seemed everyone had someone,
Except me.
I fixed romantic dinners for a man,
Who was never home.
I'd be stalked and beaten,
As he ignored my cries to leave me alone.

Now I search deep within myself.
I'm just so amazed at how my life has changed.
Those other "so-called" loves have gone away,
It just one true love that remains.

How can I not love a God,
Who will never leave me or forsake me?
Who with every need is my source and supply.

He has been my healer and my keeper,

When I suffered,

He wiped the tears from my eyes.

He has raised me up and been my strength.

Through it all, he stayed right here by my side.

He has been my truest friend,

Put his hand in my hand,

Been my guide.

I'll never love another more than this.

He is perfect in all his ways.

He is my Lord, Savior, and King,

There's a love for God,

That goes deeper than any praise.

Fantasy (Lyrical Intro)

I fell in love with a fantasy.
Since I refuse to see the real you,
I can't love me.
I've been lying to myself.
Waiting for you to do right,
Closing my heart to someone else.

But today, I shatter what is just a dream.
The next time you call-
I'll just let it ring.
What is needed must come from me.
Since I can't walk away,
Then I'll just break free.

I can't complain about you-
Over and over again,
And ruin myself for another man.
Today I'll start by loving me,
By getting myself out of this fantasy.

Hindsight   (Short Form)

Saw things I didn't believe,

But never claimed I was deceived,

Maybe I was the deceiver.

Had self-worth and strength,

But used neither.

Didn't love him,

Loved the man I thought he could be,

Failed to respect,

Who I am,

And love me.

Clear

An unblocked pathway,

Free course to love,

Cloudless decisions,

Smooth transitions,

Hearts involved in a –

Collision,

That brings smiles from above.

Garden Test

Lord what ever made you give Adam, Eve?

Was it out of his desires, or based on his need?

At noontime what did he say?

As he waited for you in the cool of the day.

Alone in the garden what did he feel?

How awesome your brief visitation, but his tears still real.

As the tigers, bears, and antelope all had their mates,

What is it that makes this creation wait?

You teach us to seek you first, and acknowledge you in everything we do,

But between each encounter that we share, there are struggles,

As we try to keep our minds on you.

For your word says, never will you leave us or forsake us,

But some sit in the garden while you make us.

Why is it something about this poem that feels like a confession?

Because in the past I've asked,

"Is there some other way to learn this lesson?"

The people no longer in the garden seem to forget,

The tears that they shed while they were being kept.

First the desert, then the wilderness, and now this garden test,

This too shall pass!

For the last will be first,

And the first shall be last.

While Waiting on You

When I can tell you I'm in love with you,

There will be a smile on my face.

Then I can finally show you those hidden feelings,

That just can't be erased.

When I can say those words and not question,

"What will be said in return?"

And feel your kisses confess, what your soul has

already learned.

When we can worship Him together,

And each night fall to our knees,

Then I'll watch the Lord send you, your heart's desire,

And you'll realize that it is me.

When I can find out who I waited for,

While each tear cried out, "Just hold on!"

Then I'll see what the Lord sent right on time,

But seemed to take too long.

When I can meet you in the park to see the sunset,
Or just stay up with you until dawn,
When I can truly experience your love day to day,
And find comfort in your arms.

See, the woman in me feels that I'm waiting on you,
But something else inside is relieved.
It was Him who was here,
While I was waiting on you,
And He's better than I would have ever believed.

Who I am, and Where We Stand

I want to prove to you that I am your rib,

Make up for every relationship that you've had that

was short lived.

I was taken from you to be the one who gives,

To give everything you need, return it all back to you,

To support you through all you have to face, and

everything that you'll go through.

To show you are a King to those still struggling to see

you as a man and

Wanting to treat you like a boy,

I have what you need, want, desire, and enjoy.

I'm not just your friend. I'm the one who will fight

every one of your foes.

I'll help you get a yes when the world has told you no.

I've mastered encouragement just to speak to your spirit,

I'll pray secret prayers over you, that would make you cry if you could hear it.

I'm the one that God has sent and ordained,

To acknowledge and be attracted to your gifts and greatness,

Even if it never leads to money or fame.

To me you are poetry,

Word play written in dope lines,

You make me happy to tell the world that you're mine.

Rough Around the Edges

Let me kiss your roughness,

Sand it down to gentleness.

Let me make your untouchable,

Quiver inside my caress.

This time,

I'm going to take my time to undress.

I'm not undressing to get down to bare skin.

I'm bearing all to you,

Not as my lover,

But as my friend.

My Warrior

There's a different type of foreplay,
Where being mentally stimulated and intrigued is
better,
Than being teased.
My ears wait for the words that
Fall from his lips.
I lean in to hear him, as if being
Kissed.

He hears what I don't say,
Not just reading between the
Lines.
Something more divine,
God-like, God's prototype,
Made in his image.
Royalty from Lineage, kingly, priestly.
My queenliness makes me run to him.
I beseech thee.

As we spend time, my purpose and opportunity align.
He uplifts me. He pours into me.
When I feel too full to move,
He tips me, and sips from me,
As if I am a glass.
So don't think you'll get his attention with just a big ass.

He is in tuned and consumed.
He values my gifts, and even
Though he loves to see it utilized,
He hides it like a secret treasure,
From a world of negativity and false measures.

He tells me that I will be great.
There's a sparkle in his eyes.
As he looks at me, he is proud.
I hear encouragement even when
He doesn't speak it out loud.

His tactics are systematic, and

His attachment is not based on the physical.

It is something spiritual.

An outward touch can never

Compare to what he has done on

The inside of me.

He is my inspiration.

He has gone deeper than any

Man, without penetration.

I give him my monogamy, and it

Has nothing to do with my body.

I admit that he is God given to be

My encourager.

God wins my battles using him

As my warrior.

Young Love

Unguarded,

Smiling,

Phone in hand,

Unplanned,

Watching his eyes,

Examine me,

Praising and appraising,

Me like jewelry,

He values me.

Equally,

As I value myself,

Knowing my own worth,

Not afraid of hurt,

Heart uncontrolled,

His heart,

Pure gold,

He handles me,

Carefully,

I don't have to,

Question his intentions,

He never fails to,

Mention me,

Like his heart and thoughts,

Set on me by default,

Others have unlocked,

My heart,

He unlocked my vault.

Young love is-

Far from robbery.

It is the reason,

I give him all of me.

True Love

True love is the power that allows you to acknowledge your faults, get over past disappointments, and move from preconceived expectations to faith.
True love is the covering that allows you to stand despite stones that are thrown.
True love is the sound that breaks the silence of past failed attempts with the harmony of acceptance.
True love is the embrace that soaks up tears and makes up for lost years.
True love is the passport that takes you through the pain of deserted places,
Seemingly impassible terrain,
Dark corridors,
Turbulent storms,
And rests you,
In a place called,
Peace.

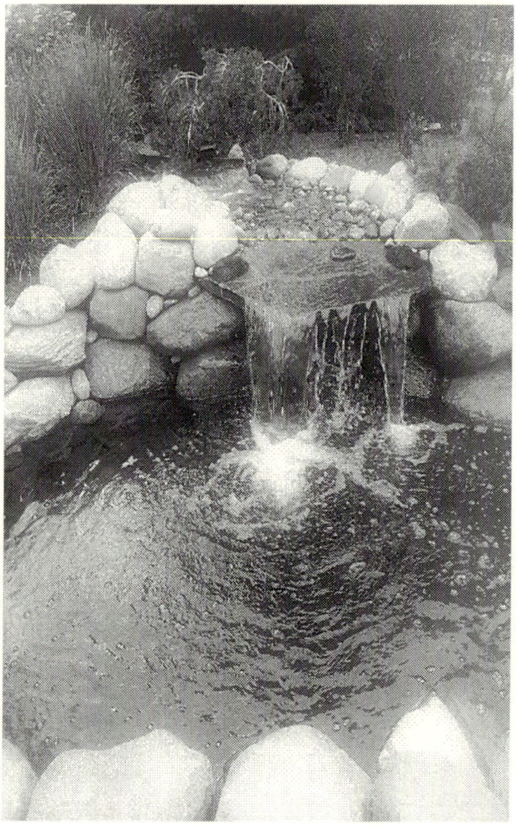

Dear King

I witnessed you bare witness,

To a love that you thought was directly from your wish list,

Her disregard for your feelings-

Relentless.

She simply wasn't ready for love.

She was argumentative and insecure,

You gave her all of you,

But she still wanted more.

Because she wanted you to pay for what others had done.

You spent time with her, but she was always on your heels,

Because she needed to heal,

I thought to myself,

I've seen this scene so many times before,

Jealousy rose up every time you were away from her.

She was money hungry,

More concerned about her bills,

Than what you both can build together,

More unstable than the weather,

Whether, or not she knew you were doing all you could,

So, I knew she wasn't the one for you.

That love isn't the same,

As what a real woman has to give,

The love that will make your life worth living,

And "L-I-VE" to live!

Some Queen is waiting on what she,

Looks at as her hand-me downs,

Because it takes a Queen,

To straighten up your crown.

Letter to Black Fathers

Today I wouldn't dare try to take your shine,
In fact, I'll be the first to admit your job is harder than mine.
You struggle to live in a world that would rather see you fail than to succeed,
Because fatherless children are easier to deceive.

The world wants your children to miss out on your direction and wisdom.
Then applaud the women for the nurturing, and love that we give them.
But today, I confess I can't do this alone.
Your son, your daughter would be devastated if you were gone.

Thanks for staying when others have tucked tail and run away.

Ignore the shots that will be fired by bitter women today.

Being a black father didn't come with a job description.

Many of you didn't have that role model, but that's one fact we fail to mention.

It must be hard to try to do what you have never,

Seen first -hand, and stand-

Being a black father, and a hell of a man.

Letter to My Teenage Son

Sometimes love wears disguises.

Hurt is like sunglasses to eyes,

Hurt hides it,

But trust me it is there.

Don't forget why you were made.

It wasn't by mistake.

Although, I'm not the type of mother that applauds your mistakes,

Don't let my broken heart and looks of disappointments make you,

Back up from me until you find yourself alone.

Go back to the love I've already shown.

I'm not raising you to be a man who never cries.

That is toxic masculinity.

The world lied.

You will cry, because you will have some bad times.

Times when you are afraid, but I love you.

Don't ever think I am better off without you,

Don't say that it is better to end it,

Than to go through what you will go through.

Son, because I know life,

I know there will be a time when you can't stand me,

And I'll question do I even know you.

I loved you before you were even aware of my touch.

Ever heard my voice,

So killing yourself,

Is not a choice!

I can't allow you to end it,

When my love for you is endless.

I don't want to ever have to say I laid my son to rest.

I don't want to question,

If I did my best.

The Holidays

The holidays are the final show after all the dress rehearsals for pain.

It's a breaking point for the accumulation of heart ache.

A culmination resulting in complete disdain.

Every riff, wedge, and argument,

Gets to torment as it resurfaces,

It's when suicidal demons, get to whisper-

You're worthless.

It's when the pain of everyone you miss, gets to be magnified,

It's when the addiction that you have,

Comes out from the place where it hides.

Months and years of sobriety,

Gets swallowed, smoked, or shot up,

You just needed one moment of relief,

Told yourself "WTF".

But today, I take back the destructive power of the

holidays.

Think about the strength it took you,

Just to make it,

Today.

Your life is worth living!

You can't give up!

Those who have gone onto heaven are looking down.

If you can close your eyes and ears to the pain long enough,

You'll find peace all around.

There are things you must go through,

I won't pretend life fixes itself instantly,

But if you could only get a glimpse of the end of your story,

You'd stay tuned, to see what the end would be.

Nighttime Praise

In the stillness of the night no one's voice can be heard,
Except the sweetest uninterrupted praises,
The chirping of the birds.

During the nighttime, you anoint their mouths to call up the dawning,
Of a brand- new day.
And my nighttime sufferings, begin to fade away.
The first appearance of light, darkness retreats, and the heavens break,
This is the glory that no man can ever take.

Everything sleeps until the Master calls,
For you are the true author and finisher of it all.
How can we let the chirping of the birds precede our praise?

When in God's image we are wonderfully and fearfully made.

How long will you wait Father, for your nighttime praise?
A victorious shout, showing we're more than conquerors over our yesterdays.

Such a humble King,
Waiting patiently on His throne.
But now Lord, I awake to honor you and you alone.

From Mere Clay

I started out as marred clay,

Destroyed by the workings of sin.

Unable to be restored,

I had to be transformed or made over again.

Lord, I need your grace and mercy,

For without you, I'm unable to stand.

The only way I can make it,

Is if I am placed in your hands.

Speak to me Jeremiah!

Tell me what the Lord allowed you to see.

The one on the wheel,

Did you recognize it was me?

Lord, spin me around,

I'll endure every test and trial.

Counting it all joy,

I shall see his complete handiwork,

After a while.

Some things I don't understand.

Like the tools that you use to shape and mold.

I heard to whom much is given, much is required,

Now I believe what I was told.

What pot can speak to the Potter?

A creature asking the Creator, why.

Though you slay me,

I am yielding,

Wiping away the tears from my eyes.

I started out in the miry clay,

Useless and not fit for it all.

I found myself,

Planted on a Rock,

Answering to his call.

Intervention

Before you were born inside of the hospital room,
I held you in the palm of my hand,
Even placed you in your mother's womb.
I spoke life to you and declared what your end would be.
Your mother hadn't felt your first kick,
But I had my eyes on thee.

I smiled and laughed, as I watched you grow,
And I saw you take your first steps.
I didn't let you die,
Because my promises had to be kept.

When you strayed away, some people felt your whole life was lost,
But I knew the paths you would take, and I decided to pay the cost.
I didn't turn away from you.

I knew it was a phase that would not last.

I patiently waited for you to follow the footsteps of my path.

So, don't be ashamed.

Hold your head up, and don't give in.

You have a new life, replace those old memories,

Because your sadness must come to an end.

There is a reason that you made it,

I have given your life purpose,

It's your destiny.

You shall be used for my glory!

That is why I made you just for me.

Outrageous Hope

I open up the curtains inside

My mind.

I didn't realize I'd left

So many darkened rooms,

Hidden chambers lacking visitors,

I guess that's what they call

Being close-minded.

I'm determined to find those vacant places.

The places where rays of hope

Bringing in the brightness of dreams,

Refuses to shine.

I open the curtains inside my mind.

My mind will be a sponge,

That soaks up the sun.

An outside source shall come

With its brilliance,

Then find its way to my fireplace,

Where embers are still burning,

Glowing,

Still strong enough to ignite,

An even brighter flame.

This time, I tear the curtains

Inside my mind.

I will never,

Be consumed with darkness

Again.

Believe

Sometimes it's hard to allow your heart to believe,

When you really want to receive,

Those things you want and need.

You've seen it happen for others,

Even believed it would happen for them,

But when you think about your turn,

It's hard to believe it will happen again.

"Just believe," sounds so simple,

The words are so easy to say,

But heartbreaking to the person,

Trying to push doubt out of belief's way.

It Will Come

Increased expectations will hasten your relief.

Your increase will come,

When doubt is defeated by your beliefs.

Forget how you've been hindered,

Walk in faith and just believe.

He that shall come,

Will come,

Don't allow delay to deceive.

You may feel somewhat held back,

Held up,

Struggling to find your way,

But you will receive your blessing real soon,

It just might be today.

Draw Nigh

Be not far from me,

I wait for those to seek me while I may be found.

Put away your shoes from your feet,

For you are standing on holy ground.

Come boldly unto my throne,

And be met with my brilliant glory as a sweet long caress.

Can you love me for just being God?

Then worship me and serve me in the beauty of holiness.

People come to me who are in need.

For many are the afflictions of the righteous,

They will suffer for my name's sake.

But who will bring a gift unto me?

Come tell me I'm worthy and give me thanks.

I sit here waiting on you,

Who will be the first to make it through the door?

To come into my presence,

And tell me again, "Lord you are the one that I adore!"

I've already heard you praise me,

I kept my promise and came down to be in the midst.

But who will draw nigh to me,

Close enough to receive their kiss.

In Your Presence

How do I get in your presence?
I'm consumed yet approaching the flame.
How do I handle your grandeur?
So unworthy, yet called by your name.

What do I do in your presence?
Lifting my hands, I tremble inside.
They don't understand my story, or-
Comprehend the tears that fall from my eyes.

How can I stand in your presence?
Surrounded by glory, and not knowing what to do.
So I reverence you, awesome and holy, and-
Humbly bow before you.

I've found myself in the midst of a river.
At first my thanks were my wading place,
But now my spirit has drifted into worship,

Searching the depths of the waters for a glimpse of your face.

You've been seen at the mount, and-

Yes, at Calvary.

You've descended from on high like a dove.

But at this moment you're right here with me,

My soul has found who she loves.

Face to Face

What will I do when I see your glory?

Shining so brightly the sun becomes grieved,

Refusing to shine.

When I can walk so close behind you,

I can't separate your footsteps from mine.

What shall I do?

Spend my forever telling you thank you,

Give you an eternity of worship from my knees.

Would it be even more awesome than I can imagine?

But just the thing, my soul knows and believes.

When I can see the one, who spared me,

Please give me enough grace to express my gratitude.

I've spent all this time,

Yearning-

For just one chance,

To be face to face with you.

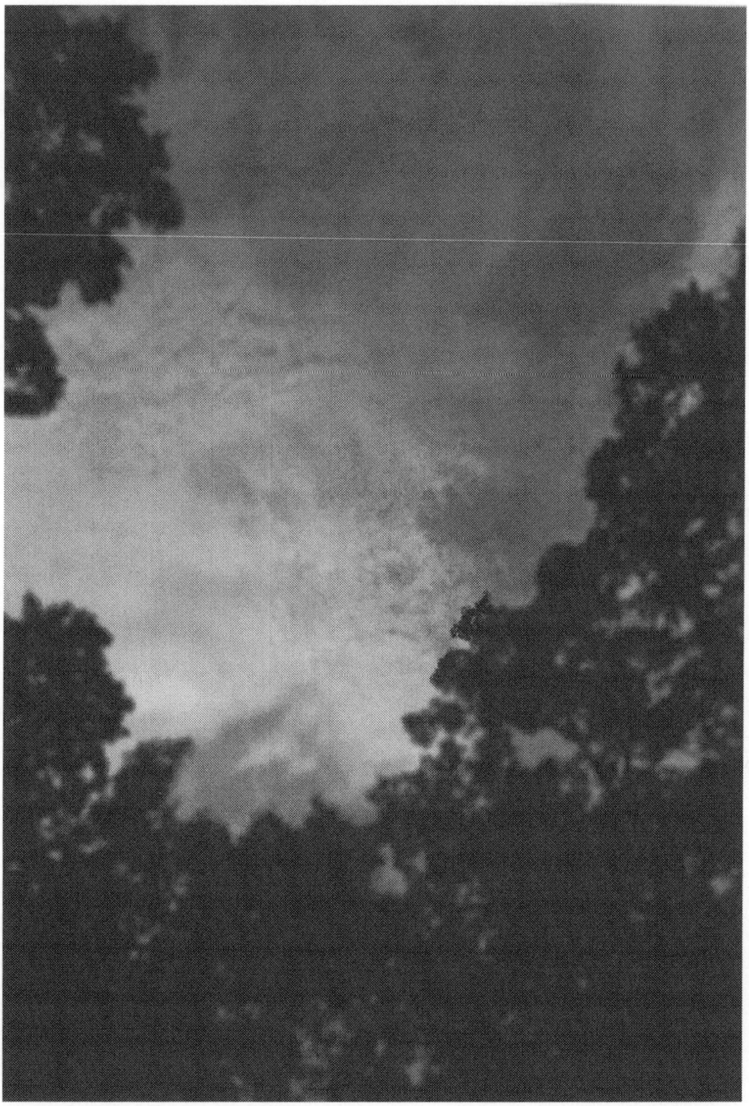

He Visits Me

When you enter sometimes it's the sweetest fragrance,

Just something in my spirit that bows down inside of me,

A fire that rests upon my head,

A glory cloud so thick I cannot see.

Sometimes you appear to receive my worship.
To delight in me giving you thanks and blessing your name.
Sometimes you just show up and show out.
Bringing me the first and the latter rain.

You come to speak to me through your word.
To confirm publicly what you've told me privately.

How can I be worthy of your presence?

Why are you so mindful of me?

There have been times when I longed to feel you near me.

Although you spoke not a word,

I had to believe my prayers made it through.

I decided; I will still seek thee.

Who would have known-

Then, I'd be visited by you.

Healed While in Worship

I stand with a bowed down head,

Symbolizing I've come before a King.

I know within myself,

There is a request that I must bring.

Met by the glory of your presence,

I fall down to my knees.

With my whole heart,

I begin to exalt you,

Reverencing your sovereignty.

My body cries out in pain,

I am frail and have grown weak.

I step beyond this condition,

Knowing there's a God of all power that I can still seek.

I can't wait on test results, or another doctor to examine me,
Lord, look upon me now.

For I have come,
That you would loose me and set me free.

I lift up my hands to thee, eyes upon the hills,
Watching and waiting for you.
I'm in need of such help,
Now one else can bring me through.

I wait for the words from your lips,
After, I've touched your hem and worship at your feet.
"You are made whole," you'll say,
"Be it unto you just as you believed."

Life's Circumstances

When your life's not in your hands,

You can't change the circumstance.

Just look to God and understand,

That it's for your good despite the plan.

Made in the USA
Columbia, SC
05 September 2019